ART and
INVENTION

Inventions in Reading and Writing

From Calligraphy to E-readers

Cory MacPherson

Cavendish Square

New York

Published in 2017 by Cavendish Square Publishing, LLC
243 5th Avenue, Suite 136, New York, NY 10016

Cataloging-in-Publication Data

Names: MacPherson, Cory.
Title: Inventions in reading and writing: from calligraphy to e-readers / Cory MacPherson.
Description: New York : Cavendish Square, 2017. | Series: Art and invention | Includes index.
Identifiers: ISBN 9781502622990 (library bound) | ISBN 9781502623003 (ebook)
Subjects: LCSH: Writing--History--Juvenile literature. | Printing--History--Juvenile literature. | Books--History--Juvenile literature. | Written communication--History--Juvenile literature.
Classification: LCC Z40.M33 2017 | DDC 411'.7--dc23

Editorial Director: David McNamara
Editor: Caitlyn Miller
Copy Editor: Nathan Heidelberger
Associate Art Director: Amy Greenan
Designer: Joseph Macri
Production Coordinator: Karol Szymczuk
Photo Research: J8 Media

The photographs in this book are used by permission and through the courtesy of: Cover Scott Eells/ Bloomberg/Getty Images; p. 6-7 Anselm Feuerbach/File:Plato's Symposium - Anselm Feuerbach - Google Cultural Institute.jpg/Wikimedia Commons; p. 10 Grotte de Pech Merle, Lot, France/Index/ Bridgeman Images; p. 15 LACMA/File:Tablet with Cuneiform Inscription LACMA M.79.106.2 (3 of 4).jpg/Wikimedia Commons; p. 18 ARCHITECTEUR/Shutterstock.com; p. 21 BabelStone/File:British Museum Flood Tablet.jpg/Wikimedia Commons; p. 25 Michael Burrell/Alamy Stock Photo; p. 26 Werner Forman Archive/Bridgeman Images; p. 30-31 Kadirkaplan/iStock/Thinkstock.com; p. 38 VLADJ55/ Shutterstock.com; p. 41 Public Domain/File:Cai-lun.jpg/Wikimedia Commons; p. 42 INTERFOTO/ Alamy Stock Photo; p. 44 -45 Buddhika Weerasinghe/Getty Images; p. 52 Universal History Archive/ UIG/Getty Images; p. 54 ViewStock/Getty Images; p. 56-57 British Library/File:Diamond Sutra of 868 AD - The Diamond Sutra (868), frontispiece and text - BL Or. 8210-P.2.jpg/Wikimedia Commons; p. 59 China Photos/Getty Images; p. 66 Carsten Koall/Getty Images; p. 69 Paul Morris/Bloomberg/Getty Images; p. 71 Peter Foley/Bloomberg/Getty Images; p 74-75 John Blyberg/File:Evolution of Readers.jpg/ Wikimedia Commons; p. 80 Hadrian/Shutterstock.com; p. 82 Courtesy Astohaus; p. 85 Courtesy Google; p. 94 Courtney Boyd Myers/File:Courtbean's Kindle Fire.jpg/Wikimedia Commons; p. 95 Joshua Keller/File:Gutenberg Bible, New York Public Library, USA. Pic 01.jpg/Wikimedia Commons.

Printed in the United States of America

CONTENTS

INTRODUCTION:
Shaping the Written Word

Where did writing come from? How has it changed people's lives? Has it always changed them for the better? The conversation about written language in Plato's famous dialogue *Phaedrus* is the perfect place for us to start our investigation of how reading and writing have evolved over time. Plato's text is an exchange of ideas between two characters, Socrates and Phaedrus. Modes of scientific investigation—reflecting, observing, and questioning the usefulness of the invention of writing—are modeled through the structure of a dialogue. Artists and inventors use this process, too. Both scientists and artists seek to make sense of the natural world. To better understand the night sky, a scientist will look through a telescope to see the stars more clearly; a writer will recreate the sky through a carefully worded description. Knowledge gives both of them the power to shape the way we perceive the world: through the lens of a telescope, we see Earth revolving around the sun; from the words of a poet, we see the moon as a symbol of mystery, melancholy, and change.

Plato used his two characters to articulate two major ways written language changed our perception of the world. Phaedrus says, "But when they came to letters, This, said Theuth [an Egyptian god], will make the Egyptians wiser and give them better memories; it is a specific both for the memory and for the wit." Here, we see that written words are a certain form of magic. The reader and writer travel through time and space to meet on the page. Simple markings are able to convey whole universes, vivid characters, and life-changing ideas. The written signs of ancient civilizations had many functions, especially remembrance of the past: inscriptions on tombs remember and honor the dead, and the painted outlines of hands on cave walls were the earliest way to say, "Remember me." And so it is: when we read their inscriptions, they are remembered.

But we can't live in the past, and in the dialogue, Socrates argues that writing is not an advancement in man's consciousness. On the contrary, he believes that reflecting upon an event and then writing about it diminishes the actual experience and removes us from the present moment:

> O most ingenious Theuth, the parent or inventor of an art is not always the best judge of the utility or inutility of his own inventions to the users of them. And in this instance, you who are the father of letters, from a paternal love of your own children have been led to attribute to them a quality which they cannot have; for this discovery of yours will create forgetfulness in the learners' souls, because they will not use their memories; they will trust to the external written characters and not remember of themselves. The [invention] you have discovered is an aid not to memory, but to reminiscence, and you give your disciples not truth, but only the semblance of truth; they will be hearers of many things and will have learned nothing; they will appear to be omniscient and will generally know nothing; they will be tiresome company, having the show of wisdom without the reality.

A symposium is a method of collective investigation most famously described by the philosopher Plato.

Written language *does* extend our memory by recreating the original experience. But we cannot attach a value judgment to it as Plato's characters have, just as we cannot look at the world only through a telescope or think of the world only as a collection of symbols. We need multiple perspectives. The earliest innovators of writing technologies saw the power of writing and used their creative energy to make a science of improving that art. Their inventions became tools, used to shape the way we experience, express, and remember the world.

INVENTIONS That SHAPED the WRITTEN WORD

The inventors discussed over the course of this book profoundly changed the way we communicate. Writing is of critical importance throughout civilization: how we read and write is how we transmit our ideas. In order to improve how we create and distribute writing, they had to create new technologies that matched their visions. **Calligraphy**, paper, the printing press, and the e-reader are all important markers in the history of writing.

At the outset of the written word, calligraphers used pens and brushes to make art of surpassing beauty, art that also communicates effectively. The development of paper as we know it allowed writing to be more widely and economically distributed, setting the stage for the printing press. And the printing press changed the course of history, sparking the rise of nations, the scientific method, and the idea of the individual. Some scholars believe it is the most important invention in human history. Today we often take it for granted, but the printing press remains a cornerstone of modern society. Finally, the Kindle e-reader marks both a change and an evolution in the story of writing, as it replaces the physical text with a digital equivalent. With each step, we see artists and innovators pushing the boundaries of what is possible, creating the foundation for the rich reading experiences that exist today.

In the digital age, we write and read more than ever before. Much of that writing is typed on keyboards, and much of that reading is done on screens. It's hard to see how these processes connect to an ancient Chinese calligrapher in a simple room, sitting before a piece of blank paper, preparing himself to make swooping strokes across its surface. Even paper itself can seem archaic in our digital world. Compared to a modern copy machine that can reproduce pages at a rapid-fire rate, the printing press appears ancient. But we must not dismiss these early inventions. Each was a link in the chain of progress. They were entirely revolutionary in their time, and the book you hold in your hands (or read on your screen!) would be impossible if just one of these inventions had never been created.

Over the next six chapters, we'll trace reading and writing from the earliest recorded humans through the innovators of today. We'll explore how writing is not confined to books, but instead is a fundamental way of expressing ourselves in our day-to-day lives. Along the way, we'll see that necessity is truly the mother of invention— and that invention is a process filled with failure, new attempts, and revisions—much like the act of writing itself.

Thanks to prehistoric cave drawings found in France, we know that writing has been essential to the human experience for seventeen thousand years.

CHAPTER 1
Early Forms of Communication

The technology we use today makes communication so effortless that we can be in constant contact with each other. With the press of a few buttons, we can send a message to someone who is in a different room, in a different house, or even in a country on the opposite side of the planet. Around 6,500 languages are currently spoken, and thousands of them have a developed writing system. The language barriers of the past have been broken; our methods of communication have advanced so that we can understand what someone is saying, even if we don't know their language.

Drawings of animals and a pattern of dots engraved on cave walls from France have been dated back to the most recent Ice Age, around 15,000 BCE. We can only guess what the cave writers were trying to say, but their inscriptions are proof that humans have a primitive need to communicate.

We have used language for millions of years. The first humans communicated using speech, so there is little physical evidence that gives us a definitive history of how and why language was formed. However, scientific study informs our understanding of language formation as part of a natural evolutionary process, instead of the quick flip of a switch that suddenly activated language in our brains.

It seems that language may not be a human invention that sets us apart from other animals, but a shared behavior that connects us to animals as pieces of a larger whole. The way we organize words to form phrases and arrange those phrases to make sentences, or **syntax**, is an important convention that other species use. Birdsong and whalesong also use syntactical organization; their songs are not composed of a series of random notes. Instead, the notes follow a specific order, arranged and repeated to make a song. Each pod of whales has its own unique music that establishes a communal identity and serves to ensure pack preservation. We can see the significant role language plays in self-identification—upon hearing whale song, a lost whale is able to identify itself as a part of the pod and can follow the call to find its way back home to safety. This idea is helpful to our understanding of early human language. Warning calls, attack calls, and mating calls equate to actions. We have always spoken to connect with other humans in the context of a group; therefore, language helps us express and understand who we are in relationship to others.

The EVOLUTION of LANGUAGE

From whalesong to wolf howl, from mating call to warning, systems of oral communication are a part of nature, expressing the primal instinct to avoid danger, to reproduce, and to eat. At its core, communication is about survival. Our first verbal exchanges communicated messages like, "I am going to attack you," or "I want to mate with you," or "The river has plenty of fish right now." Speaking was a part of our evolution as animals, and we used this skill to ensure the continuation of the human race.

The evolutionary function of language is further supported by the similar ways humans and animals use sound to make meaning. For example, when a vervet monkey vocalizes a clacking sound, other vervet monkeys will stand upright and inspect the ground. This is because vervet monkeys assign a specific meaning to a sound. The clacking sound, or "chuttering call," is a warning that a python is near. The vervet monkey's warning calls are specific; they have different calls to distinguish the presence of a python from an eagle or a leopard. This is a sophisticated version of a basic system—many animals have calls. Their calls are specific in the sense that they use one sound for warning calls and a different sound for mating calls, but the warning call announces only the general presence of danger and not its type. Like the vervet monkey, early humans used **phonetics**, or the association of sound and meaning, to form words in speech and writing. The English alphabet is an example of phonetics; each letter represents a sound.

Another theory, based on scientific research on **language acquisition** in children, suggests language began as a way to name objects. A child's first one hundred words are most commonly the names of objects or actions, like "milk" or "eat." After simultaneously hearing the name of an object ("dog") and seeing the physical object (a toy dog) many times, a child will learn to associate the word with its meaning. The child then applies it to the object type (all dogs). This evidence supports the conclusion that naming is our primary method of developing language and, most likely, was the way we developed language as a species. According to this theory, language was the skill of an evolved brain—the way to achieve higher levels of consciousness, rather than a mechanism of survival. However, with a shared language we are able to form communities. Strength in numbers and group protection are mechanisms of survival for our entire species.

Comparing these theories, we can see the relationship between a word and its function takes two different forms. We will see the different ways utility (usefulness) influenced **aesthetic** design (design that takes beauty into account) as we examine the artistic and scientific inventions across time and culture. The theory that language began as a series of survival calls is an example of the importance of function over form: the sounds used to make words did not need to be beautiful, they just needed to be distinct. On the other hand, language as a tool for observation places less emphasis on the utility of language, leaving more room for creative freedom in word formation.

LANGUAGE TAKES SHAPE

The origins of written language are not attributed to one specific date or location. Instead, we have scattered artifacts that obscure the history of language, leaving us no continuous sequence of events. As we discuss the origins of writing, it is important to point out that there are three common characteristics of written words from every language: design, sound, and meaning. This set of characteristics will serve as a guide and allow us to see connections between language development in different times and places.

Cuneiform

Cuneiform, the oldest script, dates back to Mesopotamia in 3200 BCE. Sumerians cut the ends of reeds, which are grass-like plants, and used their sharp edge to engrave characters on clay tablets. Archaeologists have discovered around four thousand tablets, a collection that tracks the two-hundred-year evolution of the script. What began as

Only a few hundred scholars can read and translate cuneiform today.

pictographs, or picture-like symbols that represent words, gradually simplified to signs that used a combination of line and wedge shapes. Almost all of the cuneiform tablets from this time were clerical records; the rest were transcriptions that were most likely made by students learning to write. These first documents were purely functional: in Mesopotamia, writing was a utilitarian development intended for practical matters. Because cuneiform script became less ornate and more practical in design over time, we can conclude that Sumerians later valued a word's efficiency over its aesthetic quality.

Hieroglyphics

Another one of the oldest recorded scripts comes from Egypt and originated approximately two centuries after cuneiform. Though both hieroglyphics and cuneiform evolved from pictographs into signs, the two scripts look very different. The hieroglyphic script has an artistic quality. By design, many of the characters are representative (or symbolic), so they look more like pictures than the abstract signs of cuneiform. In Egypt, writing was expressive, and hieroglyphics were used to mark the cultural significance of a person, place, or event. Early evidence of this script has been found on tombs, goods, and pottery as inscriptions that mark names and dates. Hieroglyphics have also been found on documents of ceremonies and royal seals. Historians speculate that writing was used to transcribe the culture's oral history and to preserve traditions.

Perhaps the most remarkable quality of Egyptian writing is how it was concerned with memory, the idea that the text would outlive Egyptian society and had a farther reach in the universe. Inscribed on tombs, writing also had a spiritual function—it was a way to communicate to the afterlife. This grasping quality, the contemplation of big concepts like existence, identity, and memory, is part of the artist's quest and is another recurring concept in the development of writing.

Hanzi

The Chinese script, **Hanzi**, is the oldest surviving form of writing, and its durability comes from the character formation. Chinese calligraphers used graphs as a means of reproducing and producing writing. But what distinguishes the Chinese from the Western and Islamic calligraphic industry was what they wrote—or rather drew—in these graphs's boxes: picture-like characters. And these were not meaningless or insignificant pictures. Each picture symbolized an idea. Therefore, those inventing the characters had to rely on their creativity and imagination. These writers associated simple pictures with complex ideas. For example, the early Chinese character for the word "sun" was made in its likeness: a circle with a small line in its center. Unlike the Sumerians and Egyptians, the Chinese developed pictographs into characters that represented words, and their entire writing system was composed of **logograms**. A logogram is a symbol that represents a word, like 7 represents the word "seven." Because this system was so efficient and easy to learn, writing caught on quickly; China was the most literate and advanced civilization in its time. As written language evolved, writers never ceased to improve upon the design, though the improvements were not because the symbol was unclear. Rather, new characters for words like "sun" were developed because later writers felt inspired to express themselves.

Over time, the symbols evolved into more intricate characters that are still used today. Each symbol is meticulously designed and made. Even the exact number and exact arrangement of brushstrokes is predetermined. Aspiring calligraphers were first required to learn that number and arrangement, and then execute it flawlessly.

Alef
[A]
bull, ox

Beth
[B]
house

Gimel
[G]
stick/camel?

Daleth
[D]
door

Héh
[E]
breath/window?

Waw
[W]
fork, crook, peg

Zaïn
[Z]
arrow, sword

Heth
[H]
wall, fence, field

Theth
[Θ/Th]
wheel

Yodh
[Y]
hand

Kaph
[K]
palm/plant?

Lamed
[L]
goad, whip

Mem
[M]
water

Nun
[N]
snake, eel

Samekh
[S]
fish/support?

Ayïn
[O]
eye

Péh
[P/Ph]
mouth

Tsadi
[C/Ts]
hook/papyrus?

Kof
[Q/Kh]
axe

Resh
[R]
head

Shin
[Š/Sh]
tooth

Taw
[T]
mark

The Phoenician alphabet was easy to learn because each symbol represented a sound.

The standard style script is characterized by its aesthetic harmony. Hanzi demonstrates the advantages of the brush as a writing tool; Chinese writers were able to develop many variations of the script to serve different purposes with different brushstroke techniques. Styles include an easy-to-read clerical script for documents and a running script that is characterized by fast brush movements which encouraged creativity and gave the impression of beauty and ease. With a script that was at once flexible and durable, it is no surprise that almost all of the earliest inventions in reading and writing took place in China.

The ABC's of ABC

Even though other civilizations began writing thousands of years before China, the next breakthrough didn't occur until around 1700 BCE, when the alphabet system was formed.

Cuneiform contained seven hundred characters, and while the hieroglyphic system had less by half, there was no fixed arrangement or combination of symbols to make words, making both languages extremely challenging to write and understand. The most significant alphabet, the Phoenician alphabet, was influenced by cuneiform but primarily used elements of hieroglyphs to create a phonetic system. Instead of using visual representations to transcribe a word, in a phonetic system each symbol represents a sound. The Phoenician alphabet is the ancestor of almost all alphabetic writing systems, including English. Developed around the eleventh century BCE, the twenty-two letters represented consonant sounds and were arranged horizontally in lines to make words. These conventions made reading and writing easy to learn.

The Greek alphabet improved upon this system by adding letters to represent vowel sounds. Even though it may sound like a small change, the inclusion of vowel sounds was a significant achievement; the Greek alphabet was—and still is—the most accurate reproduction of speech. With the Greek phonetic system, letters could be combined to make sounds that weren't part of the language (for example, the combination of *p* and *h* to make an "f" sound). Because of this quality, many languages adapted the Greek alphabet.

CREATOR and CREATION

"Writer" and "writing" are abstract words that can apply to a person performing many different activities. Using the relationship between form and function, we can define the writer in one of three distinct categories.

The Writer as Scribe

Since we know the earliest writing system is cuneiform, we also know that the first "writers" were Sumerian. Like the documents they produced, they served the utilitarian purpose of transcription. For students of cuneiform writing, education began with memorizing basic syllabic signs. This was a long process; the seven hundred cuneiform characters were each made of two basic shapes. Additionally, students were required to learn the variations of the signs as well as a list of names and words that were not part of the general lexicon because they referred to people or things within a specific community. After all of this, students finally began writing. This meant spending hours copying text over and over, practicing the skill the way you practice for a spelling bee. Finally, after mastering the craft, they graduated and worked in the royal court, in agriculture, and many other areas of society to record and keep track of information. The class standing of a **scribe** varied based on the cultural context. Some scribes were members of elite society, valued as information keepers. Others belonged to royal members, like

The story of Gilgamesh was recorded on twelve tablets between the thirteenth and tenth centuries BCE.

The EARLIEST AUTHORS

The *Epic of Gilgamesh,* the earliest recorded piece of literature, was written on a tablet around 2150 BCE. The epic poem reckons with mortality, grief, and human relationships through its depiction of Gilgamesh, the main character, and his mythic quest to find the meaning of life. Literature can take many forms: poetry, personal narratives, myths, nonfiction essays, and plays are just a few examples.

The first known author, Enheduanna, wrote poetry and prayers during the third millennium BCE. She uses writing as a way to communicate with the gods in some works, and in others she writes for personal expression, articulating her dreams and fears, and describing details of her everyday life. Her words have been collected and translated from ancient tablets. Together, her forty-two devotions are titled "The Sumerian Temple Hymns." Besides being the earliest recorded author, Enheduanna is historically significant because her work gives us a rare window into the life of a woman in ancient times. While men traditionally held office as scribes and calligraphers, Enheduanna is evidence that women of power also had the ability to read and write. It is important to remember her as we study the history of reading and writing—women may have had less access to written language and less has been written about them, but they also played a part in the development of reading and writing.

property. Many scribes served their religion, copying sacred texts. In Mesopotamia, scribes served as personal secretaries of government officials and worked in the textile, shipbuilding, and transportation industries.

When the main job of a writer is to make copies of texts or speech, this writer can be called a *scribe*. A scribe is an expert on the physical components of a word and is responsible for recreating its form. This is a learned skill that does not require the writer to be generative; a scribe makes a book but does not author it. From this perspective, it's difficult to see any artistic connection. But if we think about scribes like human printers, scribes were the bridge between writer and reader. From here we see the growth of literacy and the early creation of readership.

The Writer as Artist

"Calligraphy" comes from the Greek words *kalos*, meaning "beauty," and *graphin*, meaning "to write." In Greece, *kalligraphos* referred to a person who wrote beautifully. It is this attention to the aesthetic quality of the characters that distinguishes calligraphers from scribes. In some civilizations, like Egypt and China, writers held positions of power and were regarded as artists. Their talent was the ability to design script that communicated cultural and spiritual harmony. Like artists, the work was expressive, aesthetically beautiful, and had a style that was unique to the writer as an individual. A writer who is concerned with the visual quality of character design and the stylization of script is a calligrapher. In the next chapter, we will explore the art of calligraphy in depth. But for now, it is important to mention the art of writing in script because it is a useful point of comparison. Already, the contrast between a scribe and a calligrapher gives us a better understanding of both.

The Writer as Author

Writers make art when they use words to recreate the world so that they may better understand it. To create a work of literature, the writer finds the best words to express a specific feeling, experience, or observation. It is easier to refer to this group's writers as "writers," because this is how we define writers today. This term is also appropriate because literature acknowledges that art exists in many aspects of writing—from the music and meaning of a word, to the impulse to find answers to unanswerable questions, to how the order of words together form a rhythm. An author participates in the physical act of writing and is driven to find the words that best serve their message.

READING MATERIAL

In the beginning, writing was a special skill that belonged to a small class of people. Even though reading and writing go hand in hand, the history of reading is as complicated as the origin of writing, perhaps more so. Writing was a learned skill that took years of training to master. Around the first century BCE, bamboo, silk, clay, and **papyrus** were the main materials writers used for transcription. These materials were not easily accessible and were in high demand, which made them rare. Reading, like writing, was an unusual skill.

Unification of China and the standardization of language around 220 BCE gave birth to the most literate civilization in its time. Even though literacy for the masses didn't happen in the West until around eight hundred years later, the event was equally important and inspired a period of revolutionary thinking. As author Nicholas Carr explains, "In the quiet spaces opened up by the prolonged, undistracted reading of a book, people made their own associations, drew their own inferences and analogies, fostered their own ideas. They thought deeply as they read deeply."

READERS and WRITERS of the PAST

It can be difficult to imagine a time when only scribes would ever create letters, and the rest of the population would live their lives without writing or reading. Yet, as we've seen, early cultures recognized the importance of communicating in written forms regardless of writing's limited scope. In the next chapter, we'll see how the roles of author and scribe began to overlap as societies moved from cuneiform to a script we still use today: calligraphy.

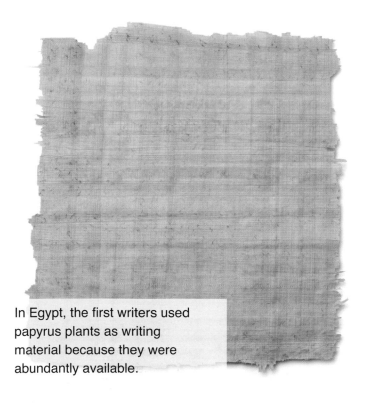

In Egypt, the first writers used papyrus plants as writing material because they were abundantly available.

Calligraphy is still practiced today and collected by people who appreciate visual art.

CHAPTER 2
Calligraphy

Historians have difficulty pointing to the exact time when humans started writing in calligraphic script. This form of beautiful writing has been practiced in every culture known to have a written language, and we still use it today for wedding invitations, diplomas, and event posters. Calligraphy enchants readers and insists we linger to notice the beauty of the text—the letters transform into art.

Ancient civilizations also used calligraphy for special occasions, like sacred texts, official correspondence, and royal decrees. In fact, ancient writers used calligraphic script as a way to show the importance of a document. Archaeologists have discovered inscriptions resembling calligraphy on ancient artifacts all over the world: bronze vessels and animal bones in China, clay pottery in Japan, and on wax tablets in Greece. Yet the origin of calligraphy is uncertain.

Without a recorded instance of invention, we will look at calligraphy and its history through a wide lens, one that enables us to view the basic human motivations that inspired the art of writing. The most distinguished styles, Western, Arabic, and Chinese, are considered the three main traditions of calligraphy. In this chapter, we will begin with a general survey of the three traditions. Each has its own cultural context, set of tools, style, and purpose.

The styles provide us with three distinct examples of the dynamic relationship that exists between aesthetics and functionality. Together, the three stories form a braided narrative about how writing developed into art.

Then we will take a closer look at Chinese calligraphy. Inscriptions found on Chinese artifacts from 2500 BCE exhibit signs of an established writing system, a highly literate population, and a set of characters that required mastery of advanced brush techniques. Many of the earliest innovations in writing developed in China, including the standardization of language, the first writing brush, paper, block printing, and primitive methods of movable type. As a result, we are able to trace the evolution of Chinese writing because its history has been so well documented and preserved.

A HOLY PRACTICE

According to tradition, the archangel Gabriel delivered a series of divine messages and revelations to the Islamic prophet Muhammad, who memorized and shared his teachings with his followers, the *huffaz*, who then taught the doctrine to their successors. Abu Bakr, the first Muslim caliph, decided his people needed a reliable and permanent way to record Muhammad's sacred teachings in order to preserve and perpetuate them. Some twenty years later, in 651 CE, the verses were transcribed, collected, and compiled into a single hand-written manuscript. Because they were so successful in their transcription and preservation endeavors, Muhammad's followers created the Islamic sacred text, the Quran, which has endured to this very day.

Kufic, the sacred script in which the Quran was originally written, is characterized by its long, bold, straight lines. Because Arabic's phonetic alphabet is devoid of capital letters and vowels, **diacritics** are also a part of the script.

Diacritics are the dots and short strokes placed above and below certain letters. With just twenty-eight letters, and seventeen basic outlines, the alphabet's simple design allowed Arabic calligraphers the artistic freedom to personalize their script. And it was the creative calligraphic liberties so many took with the alphabet's design that transformed the intended practical nature of the alphabet into an art form. More specifically, the calligraphers, who often opted to connect the letters of their script (thereby expressing artistic flair), had added an aesthetic aspect to their sacred text. The ninth century marks a highly creative period in Arabic calligraphy, as letters were decorated with leaves, flowers, and other ornamental foliage. In other cases, calligraphers artistically personalized the script to resemble a peacock.

Although nearly all these calligraphers were highly revered masters of the holy text, prestige was awarded to those artists who most accurately reproduced the scripture with precision and beauty. To reach this level of artistry, calligraphers needed to begin their training as children. However, not all children were granted this opportunity. It was only those born to families of experienced calligraphers who might one day master this sacred and prestigious craft.

WESTERN CALLIGRAPHY

An equally long-standing alphabet comes from seventh-century-BCE Rome. English, French, German, Italian, and Swahili are only a few of the many languages that use the Roman alphabet. Because it is so widely used in the Western Hemisphere, the Roman alphabet is also commonly called the Western alphabet. The letters of the Western alphabet were formed using variations of the circle and the square. The geometric composition illustrates the

This prayer was written by calligrapher Silleli Osman el-Hamdi in 1880.

بسم الله الرحمن الرحيم
اللهم انت السلام ۝ ومنك السلام
واليك يعود السلام ۝
فحينا ربنا بالسلام ۝ وادخلنا
دارك دار السلام ۝ تباركت ربنا
بالسلام ۝ وتعاليت لك الحمد

value Romans placed on mathematics. (To them, the square represented the foundation of numerical harmony.) Unlike Islamic calligraphers, these Roman writers served a practical and functional role in society. Early Roman calligraphers, for the most part, spent their time transcribing official documents, literature, and letters. This practical approach shaped the design of the Western alphabet and provided an apt form for the Roman calligrapher. It is in China, though, that we begin to see not just the convergence of writing and art, but the inextricable link between the two.

CALLIGRAPHY in CHINA

The Chinese approach to calligraphy, which, for all practical purposes, put aestheticism in a superior position, still had a lot in common with the West's primarily serviceable and sensible approach. Just as the Romans' writing had a utilitarian foundation, so too did China begin its writing system with straightforward intentions.

Yet Chinese calligraphy is more than copying complicated symbols. It is a spiritual practice, and once the basic characters are learned—at least three thousand of them—then calligraphers are free to express emotion. In fact, according to tradition, the art of writing is considered one of the "three perfections." A mastery of calligraphy, painting, and poetry is the mark of a truly cultured person. Chinese calligraphy requires skill, imagination, and training. Like a painter, a calligrapher develops his art by patiently copying and studying the work of a master. This enables him to write speedily and without hesitation, inspired by nature, as each stroke and dot of a character suggests a natural object. The goal is to give further life to words, to animate them without losing meaning.

Beginning in Bone

Inscribed on animal bones and tortoise shells beginning three thousand years ago, the Chinese "oracle-bone" script was the precursor to Hanzi. Mostly composed of pictographs, the oracle-bone script was formulaic and was used to record the names of the dead along with their dates of death or birth. There is also archaeological evidence—inscriptions made in metal, jade, and stone—that suggests the script was also used for family or clan seals.

Calligraphy Begins

Over time, the characters were developed into the earliest form of Hanzi. The new script was more aesthetically pleasing than the primitive oracle-bone script. Remember from the previous chapter that form is directly related to function? The ancient Chinese calligraphers designed the script so that it was in harmony with decorative vessels. Put another way, written language was no longer simply a primitive marking system—it was a way of expressing meaning and feeling, and the words visually communicated their meaning. From 1700 to 800 BCE, royal scribes designed a new, more stylized written form. Called the Great Seal Script, the traditional, sophisticated script of the court was used for royal, military, and clerical records, but also for ceremonial events and literature, such as poetry and long narratives.

While the royal script was elaborate and more decorative, there were too many characters and the brush strokes were too advanced for everyday use. During the fourth century CE, individual characters were redesigned to fit nearly perfect squares. It became the work of calligraphers to take the new, simplified characters and add their own artistic style. Every time they wrote, they composed their own variation of the script with each brushstroke.

Mastering the Process

Earning the title of master calligrapher was no small achievement; the aspiring calligrapher needed to be self-disciplined, talented, and passionate. Masters completed a rigorous education, which included studying traditions and techniques and spending hours each day copying transcriptions and practicing brush strokes. The muscles in their hands memorized the feel of the writing tool, its weight and dimensions. Their eyes were trained to pay attention to the nuances of language, the shapes and angles of script. Skilled calligraphers proved their mastery by using advanced stroke techniques to compose highly stylized scripts.

Nature was the inspiration for early Chinese calligraphers, and they aimed to make symbols that would provoke feelings of harmony and tranquility. The Tang calligrapher Su Qianli put it this way:

> I have seen flocks of queen swans floating on their stately wings, or a frantic stampede rushing off at terrific speed. Sometimes in a line a flaming phoenix dances a lordly dance, or a sinuous serpent wriggles in speckled fright, and I have seen sunken peaks plunging headlong down a precipice, or a person clinging to a dry vine while a whole valley yawns below. Some strokes seem as heavy as the falling banks of clouds, others as light as the wing of the cicada.

For a calligrapher, the artistic process is just as important as the final physical product. Calligraphers use a variety of brushes: hard fur brushes like weasel hair produce fine lines, and soft fur brushes like goat hair (which are more difficult to control) allow a variation in strokes. The materials used by calligraphers are sometimes called the "Four Treasures of the Study" in China. This term refers to a brush, ink, an inkstone, and paper. First, the writer rubs the inkstone, creating time for reflection and consideration of the quality and color of the ink. Next, the calligrapher visualizes the character to be formed. But it is important that the vision goes beyond just seeing the technical design. The writer must feel connected to nature before making the first brush stroke. Chinese calligraphers are, in fact, much more like modern-day painters than contemporary writers. Like painters, they use brushes, careful strokes, specialty ink and paints, and they hone their technique over time. In the end, they produce beautiful works of art.

Calligraphy was important not just for the beauty of the individual pieces created by the calligrapher, but for the way it stimulated intellectual life. Once China was unified and a standard writing system was developed, calligraphy facilitated the exchange of ideas among people and provinces. A thriving field of art criticism formed around the calligrapher's work. For example, Lady Wei Shao's treatise on calligraphy laid out aesthetic norms for the art still honored today. Calligraphy was a huge cultural shift, and as more people became literate, the flow of Chinese culture was permanently altered.

CALLIGRAPHY TODAY

As printing technologies abounded across the world and literacy increased exponentially, the importance of calligraphy began to decline, especially in the West, where their languages were a better fit for the new printing methods.

However, in the East, digital technology has failed to replace the art of handwritten calligraphy. Even after methods of printing were developed, Chinese printers still attempted to approximate handwritten manuscripts.

Books printed between 1450 and 1480 CE are almost indistinguishable from hand-lettered manuscripts of the same period. Today, calligraphers from the East honor the spiritual aspect of the ancient art. In fact, calligraphy is often practiced in monasteries. Modern calligraphers, just like those who came before them, use brush, ink, and paper to express deep emotions on the page. Besides retaining its spiritual value, calligraphy is also highly valued as an art form. Works of calligraphy are sold and collected as paintings instead of literature.

By the end of seventeenth century, the West was almost exclusively focused on the utilitarian function of writing, not the physical script. But a new role arose, not for calligraphy, but for designing the look of the type used by presses.

While the future of calligraphy is uncertain, the importance of **typography** has only increased. Today, most of the writing we see is formed by type, and the computer enables us to create and refine as many fonts as we can dream up. This means that type is increasingly unique, and typography as an art is experiencing a kind of renaissance in the graphic design world. While typographers may use digital tablet computer programs to refine their type—not a goat-hair brush and a pool of ink—the importance of how words *look*, in addition to simply what they communicate, persists. Though typing is not necessarily the meditative process that calligraphers practiced, the more attention we pay to how our words look, as well as what they express, the better we understand the art, as well as the science, of writing.

EDWARD JOHNSTON, TYPOGRAPHER

Many of the fonts designed by the earliest typographers are still in use today. The commonly used font Baskerville is now over two hundred years old. So even if calligraphers are rare these days, much attention is still paid to the form of letters and the design of type. Just as calligraphy is more complicated than "handwriting," and calligraphers have to carefully study their craft, typographers must study the different functions and purposes of certain elements of type.

In 1915, London's transport services commissioned a typographer, Edward Johnston, to design a new alphabet for publicity and signs on trains and platforms. His **sans-serif** block letter alphabet, called Johnston Sans, was meant to strike a balance between the clean readability of a sans-serif font and the traditional **serif** ones. Johnston's font inspired generations of typographers and left a lasting legacy.

In early China, writers inscribed their text on narrow strips of bamboo.

CHAPTER 3
The Invention of Paper

In the previous chapter, we saw how China was ahead of other civilizations in the development of writing and literacy. Paper fits perfectly into the litany of achievements from early China. However, paper was not just the consequence of a forward-thinking culture; unlike the Western civilizations who were writing on papyrus, a material that was plentiful and efficient, China relied on silk, bamboo, and wood. Because these materials were either cumbersome or expensive, China needed something more accessible to use.

Archaeologists have unearthed evidence that paper, in a more primitive form, existed for centuries before its date of official intervention, 105 CE. Early Chinese words for paper and descriptions of paper-like materials have been found in literature that dates as far back as 13 BCE. Fragments of specimens from northwestern China provide physical proof that paper prototypes existed in the second century BCE. However, in spite of these artifacts, historians unanimously attribute the invention of paper to Cai Lun, whose manufacturing process introduced three fundamental elements that papermakers still use today: clean water, **cellulose fiber**, and a screen mold. This degree of refinement elevated papermaking;

CAI LUN: RAGS to RICHES

According to *History of the Later Han Dynasty*, a text authored by China's official historian, Fan Ye, in the fifth century CE, Cai Lun "initiated the idea of making paper from the bark of trees, remnants of hemp, rags of cloth, and fishing nets. He submitted the process to the emperor in the first year of Yuanxing [105 CE] and received praise for his ability. From this time, paper has been in use everywhere and is universally called, 'paper of Lord Cai.'"

Cai Lun was serving as an official of the weapons and instrument manufacturing department in the Chinese court when he invented paper. He was born in 50 CE, and we can trace his inspiration back to his childhood; Cai grew up in the Hunan province, under the whispering leaves of the paper mulberry tree, an indigenous plant that later became a crucial ingredient in his paper formula. Though he began as a palace guard from a poor family, Cai became a powerful official in the imperial court after several promotions, refining his life through determination and hard work, just as he refined his invention.

A more convenient writing surface would solve a national problem, and its discovery would be a praiseworthy success. By trade, Cai was primed for such a discovery. He already had the mind of a creator, witnessing the creative process every day while he oversaw the production of weapons and instruments. By virtue of his post, his main task was to perform a thorough quality inspection, an assessment of an object in terms of craft and function. Through this process of research and problem solving, he constantly found ways to improve both the production method and the product.

Cai's post was another rung on the career ladder of an ambitious man. Because of his strong work ethic, he received a series of promotions that earned him a title of rank, raising his status from palace guard to palace official. From this vantage point, Cai could see the lack of accessible materials as an opportunity to create a new instrument for writing and, consequently, prove his talent and worth.

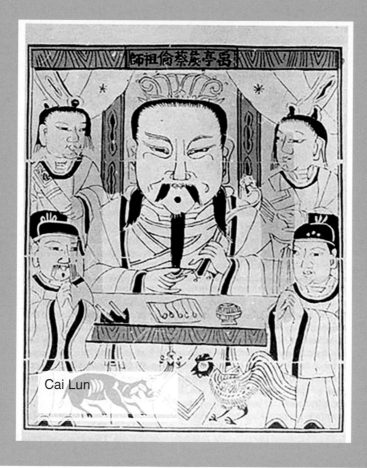

Cai Lun

To make paper by hand, papermakers use a large screen to remove water from a mixture of beaten rags and bark.

throughout history, those who create paper by hand regard their work as a form of art.

From the official Chinese historical accounts, it appears that Cai Lun invented paper for a purely practical reason: to provide the court with a convenient medium for government correspondences and records. This meant finding ways to solve the economical and physical problems that came with using bamboo and silk as writing materials. Applying scientific methods of inquiry, assessment, and experimentation to find a solution, he repeated this cycle of trial, error, assessment, and correction until he created the perfect product.

The invention may have been conceived to serve practical purposes, but Cai experimented with the papermaking process until he achieved aesthetic perfection. His aim was to create a tested method that would result in a durable writing surface every time.

In 105 CE, Cai presented the emperor with an official report that detailed the invention of paper, including instructions for its making. Although the official report has been lost, historians agree that the following is an approximation of Cai's original process: Paper mulberry bark was **felted**, or beaten into a pulp, **macerated**, and screened through fishing nets. Next, the wet mixture was applied to a flat mold where it dried to become a thin mat, called *chih*. Directly translated, the Chinese word for paper, *chih*, means "mat of refuse fibers."

The NATURE of PAPER

Without an extensive biography, we will never fully know the man who invented paper. Instead, we are left to assemble the sparse details that are available. *Dongguan Hanji*, an official account of Chinese history, says, "He was a man of talent and learning, loyal and careful. When he was off duty, he usually shut himself up and

The Japanese village of Echizen Washi is world famous for handmade paper.

refused to see visitors but exposed himself to nature." Because of the personal details, this description is useful in spite of how short it is; here, we can imagine Cai in nature, observing its beauty as he collects inspiration in solitude. Perhaps this reputation sparked the legend that Cai invented paper after watching paper wasps as they made their nests.

While this story may be myth, his choice to use organic materials was certainly cultivated by his exposure to nature. Yet Cai's solution far exceeded his intentions. Paper was a revolutionary piece of technology; its widespread use advanced communication. International correspondence and innovations like the newspaper and mass printing, for example, were facilitated by the invention of paper. Additionally, in its making, Cai discovered hydrogen bonding. The papermaking process causes a structural connection that binds hydrogen and oxygen atoms. This magnetic attraction joins the individual fibers of the pulp to form a new entity: paper. However, scientists would not identify papermaking as a chemical reaction until the 1900s, when the concept of hydrogen bonding was fully developed.

GLOBAL PAPERMAKING ROUTES

Even though papermaking was widely used in ancient Eastern civilizations, Europe did not adapt papermaking techniques until the fourteenth century. On the other hand, geography was the main reason paper made its way into Eastern cultures by the seventh century. Korea was directly influenced by China's culture; parts of the country were under Chinese control from 108 BCE until 220 CE. Geographic proximity meant that, like China, other civilizations in the East also were limited to writing on bamboo and silk before developing paper. Paper was a largely unknown technology in the West, where papyrus leaves were abundant and provided an easy-to-use writing surface.

Hanji: Korean Paper

There is no record of how and when paper was introduced to Korea, but paper specimens collected from the first century through the sixth century CE suggest that paper manufacturing began somewhere within that time period. Just like paper from China, early Korean paper was made from raw materials—such as paper mulberry, hemp, and bamboo—that were broken down into a pulp, screened through a frame, and left to dry in a mold.

However, once they mastered the process, Korean papermakers developed their own techniques to make a product that was special to their culture. Most notably, Korean paper was thick and durable, unlike the delicate sheets from China. Instead of using a top screen that controlled the thickness of each sheet, papermakers spread the fibrous pulp over the screen by hand, also referred to as the "hand scoop" technique. Additionally, Korean paper was so durable because it was dried slowly in a warm temperature, instead of quickly by fire.

Washi and *Kami*: Japanese Paper

In 610 CE, Buddhist priests from Korea introduced papermaking to Japan. Adapting Korean and Chinese techniques and adding their own rituals, the craft became a major part of Japanese history and culture; papermaking was a form of spiritual expression that created a material representation of man's connection to nature. According to Japanese tradition, paper was a gift bestowed to a prince by the "Goddess Who Lives above the Stream." The sense of divinity can also be seen in the Japanese words for paper: **washi**, paper made by hand; and **kami**, a more conversational word that refers to any type of paper. Kami is still used today, and it comes as no surprise that the word has a second meaning; kami is also used to name extraordinary spirits in nature and weather: rain, lightning, trees, and the sea.

Though the craft of papermaking has been passed down for centuries, the process has remained largely unchanged. Living fossils, papermakers have upheld tradition for a thousand years. Clean white paper is the color associated with purity and spirituality in Japan. Paper is a symbolic and physical manifestation of purity, and its color is achieved naturally from exposure to the sun. Papermakers from Japan take pride in the organic quality of their process; in some countries, handmade paper is treated with chemicals, like bleach or dye. Sun bleaching may extend the length of the process, but this is also part of its virtue—a spiritual ritual that requires patience and tranquility.

Washi is still revered in Japan today. In spite of the modern technology that enables paper production in mass quantities, papermakers still perform the ancient ritual to ensure quality and aesthetic value. Ichibei Iwano IX is one of the most esteemed papermakers; in 2002, the Japanese minister of education, culture, sports, science, and technology named him "Living National Treasure," a title that recognizes the mastery of an artist or craftsman. The nomination is also an endorsement of the entire trade of papermaking—a recognition of its longstanding history, its current cultural significance, and a call for its preservation in the future.

Parchment

Papyrus had been the primary writing material beginning in Egypt in 3000 BCE—the plants were easily bound together with water to form scrolls, long writing surfaces that could hold book-length texts. During the second century CE in Europe, parchment, or animal skin that has been treated and stretched to create a large writing surface, provided a more durable alternative to papyrus leaves. Western civilizations transitioned to paper, which was more aesthetically pleasing than papyrus leaves and less expensive than parchment, during the Islamic Golden Age (the eighth to the thirteenth century). It's likely that China introduced paper to Arab civilizations on the Silk Road, an ancient trade route that connected the East and the West.

Papermaking in the West did not require the same level of artistry as it did in the East. During the fifteenth century, a water-powered machine called a stamping mill was used to beat the cloth and bark into a pulp. First used in Spain, this technology could produce up to 4,500 sheets a day and contributed to paper's growing popularity in the West.

PUTTING PEN to PAPER

Remember that in ancient China, writing brush, ink, inkstone, and paper were named the "Four Treasures of the Study," or a calligrapher's essential materials. Calligraphy preceded the invention of paper by centuries, so paper's inclusion, instead of bamboo or silk, illustrates the influence the new medium had on the art field. Calligraphers have the skills of both the writer and the painter, and their work is valued for its content and its visual aesthetic. Paper provided artists with a beautiful medium that was able to retain the quality of brushwork. But the material did more than just meet their basic needs. Access to an abundant paper supply gave artists the opportunity to experiment and deepen their practice.

The papermaker's careful attention to craftsmanship and process provided artists with a medium that enhanced their work. One extreme example is the story of a group of craftsmen who made paper for panoramic paintings in the body of a ship. Besides capacity and length, the boat also offered a beautiful setting for their ceremonial production: the papermakers followed the rhythm of a drum to move collectively as they ran the macerated pulp through a large mold. While this is an exceptional instance, papermakers were responsive to the needs of an artist, formulating paper that enhanced the quality according to the type of ink and stylus.

The poet's first draft, the painter's sketch, the architect's cathedral plan, the scientist's process of inquiry, and the composer's song all materialize on a piece of paper. These are just a few of many examples; creative minds in nearly every discipline use paper to visualize their ideas. Claude Marks was one of the first in the art history field to study sketchbooks, a pioneer in this specific area of scholarship. Among the sweeping evidence of historical sketchbooks collected from various disciplines and individuals, Leonardo da Vinci stands out as one of the most prolific thinkers. Estimated to contain around four thousand pages of sketches, thoughts, records of brainstorming, formulations, and observations, his notebooks were an indispensable tool instrumental to his creative process. So, paper is more than just a canvas; it's also a drawing board.

Unlike China or Japan, America doesn't have a longstanding history with paper. The trade of handmaking paper died out in 1929. However, in 1971, Kathryn and Howard Clark reintroduced America to handmade paper when they opened Twinrocker Handmade Paper. The company found its niche in the art world—specialty paper was highly popular among artists who released limited print editions of their work. Even though they were new to the craft of papermaking, their artistic calling was similar to the papermakers from ancient times—their job was to produce a medium that enhanced the artist's work. Kathy Clark describes her vocation beautifully: "Practically every other craft has more design to it. Papermaking has design, too, but it's subtle and minimal, since it's there to enhance the image on the surface. It's kind of like an instrument in an orchestra: you don't see the violin in the music, but the violin is creating the sound. Papermaking is like a musical instrument—only it's visual."

A Gutenberg press

CHAPTER 4
Movable Type

I n ancient China, before printers were available, documents were reproduced manually. A pressperson applied ink to a carved block of wood. The wood block was like a large stamp: pressing the engraved characters onto a surface—most commonly clay, silk, or paper—left behind an inked impression. This process, called wood blocking, was first used in 220 CE to make imperial seals. Characters were carved in **relief**, the surroundings chiseled away to form raised marks, on small blocks of wood. Engraved characters, or **intaglio** inscriptions, carved into metal deep enough to fill with ink were another early form of print.

In 200 CE, molds inscribed with longer blocks of text enabled multiple reproductions of entire documents, facilitating book production and literacy. It was very time consuming to carve large blocks of wood with a series of characters, and the blocks themselves became useless after the initial run of prints, unless it was a text—like a royal seal—that would need to be reproduced many times. This slow production rate prohibited developments in printing. In spite of this new wood-block printing technology, documents were still copied by hand.

One of the first methods of printing was wood blocking.

The FIRST PRINTED TEXTS

Printed on a 17.5-foot-long (5.3-meter-long) paper scroll and dated 868 CE, the *Diamond Sutra* is the oldest surviving complete printed book. The Buddhist ideals about meditation, transcendence, and reaching enlightenment outlined in the *Diamond Sutra* are still part of the contemporary practice of Zen Buddhism. Because the printer's emblem included a precise date, "The fifteenth day of the fourth moon of the ninth year of Heisn-thung," and the detailed illustrations indicate a sophisticated printing technique, the *Diamond Sutra* is considered the first instance of a complete book printed with wood blocking.

The Korean *Jikji* is recognized by UNESCO as the first known book printed using metal movable type. Originally two volumes and 307 chapters, only thirty-eight pages of this text of Buddhist teachings survive today. Printed in 1377, this book represents the importance of the East in the development of print culture, while also representing how Eurocentric versions of history have tended to neglect or erase other cultures' contributions to human advancement. In fact, the *Jikji* is currently housed in Paris, France, at the Bibliothèque Nationale. It is thought that a French ambassador to Korea "collected" the book while France was at war with Korea. It was eventually donated to the national library, but it was twenty years after the donation, when a Korean assistant rediscovered it, that the true significance of the book was realized. Korean organizations have called for the *Jikji* to be returned to Korea, while French authorities maintain that the book is part of our common human history, and not specific to one culture. This argument is perhaps a bit ironic, considering how the *Jikji* is often overlooked in favor

The *Diamond Sutra*, from 868 CE, is the oldest surviving complete book printed using the wood-blocking technique.

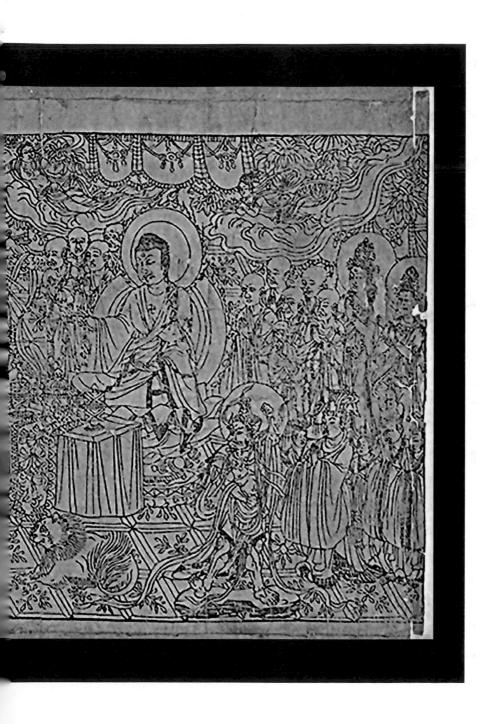

BI SHENG: MOVABLE TYPE MOVES ON

In 1045 CE, Bi Sheng had the idea to inscribe each character into a token, made out of clay, for printing. He applied wax and paper ash to an iron plate, then carefully arranged each tile side by side across the wax. After he warmed the whole plate, he could use another flat surface to press the tiles evenly into the malleable wax, ensuring that the tiles were set at a uniform depth. The ingenuity of this design solved the major problem in wood-block printing—printers no longer needed to recarve characters for each page. But China continued to use the more economical—if less efficient—wood-blocking method, perhaps partly because of the unwieldy nature of having to create and store thousands of characters for Chinese movable type, and perhaps because Bi Sheng was a commoner, not part of the imperial court. Later advances—like Hua Sui's invention of bronze movable type in 1490—were roughly parallel to the Gutenberg press. Consequently, Western historical accounts tend to overlook Bi Sheng's invention of movable type in favor of the more sensational story about Gutenberg and his revolutionary printing press. Movable type may have been an experiment at the time, but it was a major breakthrough in printing technology, instrumental to Gutenberg's press.

By virtue of location, Korea's literary development was highly influenced by China's cultural and technological advancements—Korean script and paper were both adapted from China. Around the beginning of the fifteenth century, the Korean court called for a new writing system that was easier to use than the bulky

Chinese script. Streamlined to twenty-eight fundamental signs, the new script, **Hangul**, was easier to learn and read. In order to accommodate the growing demand for books, Korea engineered a more functional version of Bi Sheng's model with durable casts made out of bronze instead of clay. A Korean Buddhist text, the *Jikji,* which roughly means "collection of Buddhist Zen teachings," was printed with metal movable type in 1377, and is certified by UNESCO as the world's oldest extant (surviving) book printed with **metalloid** type, seventy-eight years prior to Gutenberg's famous Bible. Because of this innovation, print production flourished in Korea and lay the groundwork for the future of print in the West.

Korean script, or Hangul, has a square design so that the characters can be written and read easily.

of the Western Gutenberg Bible when the history of print culture is being discussed, even though Gutenberg's Bible came nearly eight decades after this Korean text.

These early printed religious texts show the importance of movable type and print technology in spreading and cementing religious ideas. While instructions from local monks were important for Korean Buddhists, for example, the ability to read the teachings of famous monks from China, India, or other parts of Korea, neatly bound in a book like the *Jikji*, allowed adherents to deepen their faith. It also facilitated the spread of ideas. All the copies of the *Jikji* were the same. That is the point of the printing press: to standardize the copying of documents. Once an identical text can be distributed to many people, readers are free from discussing and arguing over facts and versions, and there's more room for a discussion of interpretation and opinion. In this shift, we can see how the printing press aided the rise of individuality in later ages.

FINE PRINT: GUTENBERG PRESS

In the mid-1440s, a man named Johannes Gutenberg moved to Mainz, Germany, to work on the print production of an entire Bible—a project he referred to as "secret art" and "adventure and art" to protect his methods from being stolen. Because the printing press was surrounded by secrecy, we only have an approximate date of invention: Gutenberg succeeded somewhere between 1446 and 1450. Finally revealed, Gutenberg's "secret art" could print two hundred to four hundred pages a day, had a uniform font that included upper and lowercase letters, used ink that could adhere to metal, and employed a screw press to apply force evenly and print precise characters. The printing press took nearly a decade to develop, but by the time Gutenberg opened his print shop, he had perfected his method. Though we don't know the specifics of his invention process, we can deduce from the length of time he spent on its development that the final product was refined through experimenting at every level of innovation, using trial and error to find the best possible technique. The son of a goldsmith, Gutenberg used his experience working with metal to invent a **matrix**, a carved-out letter where molten lead, once hardened, could reproduce a raised letter of uniform size and height. With a consistent method of casting type, Gutenberg created a font—a complete set of characters of the same type and size. What Bi Sheng had achieved with his wax method, Gutenberg had perfected. Printing presses continued to use his method, unchanged, for hundreds of years.

The THOUGHT of BOOKS

As we've seen in previous chapters, reading, writing, and print were all under imperial control in China. Print production was even an office held in the royal court. China, once the leader in reading and writing innovation, was slow to adopt the printing press—East Asia didn't use the mechanical printing press until the late 1800s. In early publications, books were a way to extend the power of the ruling class and distribute sacred texts. It is not without reason that Gutenberg's first book was a Bible, and that the first book printed with metal movable type, the *Jikji*, was a Buddhist text. Publishing and religion have always been deeply connected. After a millennium of technological advancements, innovation

JOHANNES GUTENBERG: The MYSTERIOUS MAN from MAINZ

Not much is known about the life of Johannes Gutenberg. Historians have cobbled together a loose timeline of Gutenberg's life using court records. The most significant of these, a lawsuit from 1439, caused speculation regarding Gutenberg's claim on the printing press. Before moving to Mainz, he lived in Strasbourg and worked with three other men on a business endeavor that involved manufacturing mirrors. During the Plague, the group fell apart, and one of the partners died. Afterward, Gutenberg was sued for the deceased member's share of the business. The court records reveal receipts of lead and frame purchases. Although there is no hard evidence that proves the partners were involved in Gutenberg's printing press, many historians conclude it was likely that the group purchased materials used for manufacturing print, not mirrors.

For all the mystery that surrounded his invention, the publication date of the Forty-Two-Line Bible, also known as the Gutenberg Bible, confirms that by 1455, his printing press was fully realized and functional. Gutenberg's Bible was a magnificent book. The work of a perfectionist, each page formed a **golden rectangle**, also known as the divine proportion (because it's often found in nature), and each page had forty-two lines of text, printed in divine proportion columns. He printed approximately forty-eight copies of the 1,286-page-long book.

in the East slowed down while civilizations in the West experienced a cultural growth spurt. The printing press was then used to challenge the power of religion, causing a revolution in individual thought in the West. Next, we'll see how books acted as channels for individuals to voice their ideas.

Pressing Questions

"Do I know how I feel? Do I know what I think?
Let me take ink and paper. Let me take pen and ink."
—T. S. Eliot

The fourteenth to seventeenth century was a period of cultural growth in Europe. The Renaissance, or "rebirth," is often remembered for the major works of art and scientific discoveries from that time, like Michelangelo's frescoes in the Sistine Chapel and Copernicus's observation that Earth orbits the sun. But the Renaissance was not just a revival of art and innovation—it was a revival of cultural identity, an evolution of human consciousness. And in its center stood the printing press. With an efficient and accessible way to print on a large scale, literacy levels grew seemingly overnight.

The printing press centralized national written languages in Europe. Unlike the government-sponsored publications in the East, Western printing was a private, commercial endeavor. Publishing houses set language standards, including grammar, syntax, and vocabulary, so that their books could reach a wider audience and make a bigger profit.

With easy access to literature, readers could independently pursue knowledge. The newly empowered reader played a major part in facilitating the age of experimentation and scientific discovery. Copernicus's *De Revolutionibus Orbium Coelestium* was printed in 1543 and introduced a model for scientific experimentation that was based on hypothesis. In *Areopagitica*, Milton argued for freedom for individuals to state their ideas in print. The growing interest in science coincided with a growing distrust of the church. Mass production of books brought the reader and writer closer together. For the church, this meant the congregation could read the Bible on their own, attaining truth by reading rather than attending church. A direct result of this new access to written scripture was the Protestant Reformation, which began when Martin Luther began to circulate his Ninety-Five Theses, a document criticizing the Catholic Church, printed on a printing press.

Increased book production also meant reading and writing were no longer exclusively for the elite. Books were no longer only reserved for the ruling classes. The rise of nationalism and a sense of national identity coincided with both the proliferation of printed books and the increased importance of the individual in Western culture. Just as people were differentiating themselves from one another while information flowed more freely than it ever had, cultures began this differentiation, leading to the system of countries we recognize today. As Latin fell out of use as the language of the intellectual elites, national **vernaculars**—English, French, German, etc.—rose to prominence, and more and more books—including the Bible—were published not in Latin, but in the author's vernacular language. This meant that the vernacular language became of increasing importance to cultures where a single language had been spoken among the elites of many cultures: Latin. As countries became more and more unified in their economies and through the sharing of information facilitated by the printing press, nationalistic pride increased. People began to feel British or Italian. Your loyalty was no longer to your class or your lord, but to your cultural group, and the idea of that culture was directly shaped by printing technologies.

The printing press was also instrumental in the rise of an entire genre of writing: the novel. Because printing was a family business, women worked in print shops and had access to literature. In the 1620s, female authors began publishing novels, personal narratives that gave voice to the writer's or character's inner life—the way an individual thinks and feels about her mind, spirit, and experiences. Mass printing changed the way we read; instead of reading religious texts in the public space of a church, people have their own copies and read in private spaces. The novel was a medium for intimate connection between the reader and writer, an invitation for the reader to enter into the author's world. Reading was at once an internalized experience and act of imagination. With mass publication of books, each reader could have his or her own individual copy to read, reread, and write in the margins. The book became a personal belonging. In the next chapter, we'll see how the Kindle e-reader allowed readers to have a personal library that was portable and accessible as a single book.

Amazon is one of the leaders in e-commerce.

CHAPTER 5
The Kindle
E-reader

After a cross-country road trip with his wife, winding his way from the corporate, hedge-fund world of New York City to the West Coast sensibility of Seattle, Jeff Bezos stepped out of the car onto the streets of Seattle with a business plan. No longer working for other people on Wall Street, he would be an entrepreneur. He already had the name for his site: Amazon.com. And he knew what he wanted to sell. Even though he had aggressive plans to expand Amazon (he also considered "Relentless" as the domain name for his website) into an "everything store" as it functions today, Bezos always knew that books would be the foundation of his empire.

BOOKS on DEMAND

As the internet age matured and e-books evolved, Bezos realized that even though he had founded his company on the idea of selling physical books directly to customers, Amazon would need to make a bold move in the direction of e-books if they wanted to stay relevant in the digital era. He tasked Gregg Zehr, the head of Amazon's division Lab126, to create a physical, portable device for reading e-books. This device would come to be called the Kindle, the first dedicated e-reader, and the first device to be seamlessly integrated with Amazon's e-bookstore, enabling readers to download a new book anywhere, at any time.

Bezos looked to Apple and realized their dominance of the MP3 player market with the iPod meant he would need to do something similar for e-books—before someone else beat him to it. But many doubted Bezos. Critics didn't believe that consumers cared as much about books as music and doubted that the general public could be convinced to buy a device just for reading books. Of course, truly disruptive technology is by definition unanticipated by most of the population; if everyone thought it was a good idea, someone would have already done it.

Because there were no other e-readers on the market at the time, the Kindle was not designed to compete with other e-readers. The device had a higher ambition: to compete with books themselves—paper, ink, and glue. The designers of the Kindle continue to see this as their goal today. Even though there are many competitors on the market now, they want their e-reader to not just be better than all the other e-readers, but to be better than reading a physical book. Bezos told his engineers, "I want you to proceed as if your goal is to put everyone selling physical books out of a job."

BEAUTY by DESIGN

As a businessman, Bezos's chief concern was creating a profitable product. He may not be an artist, but Bezos paid great attention to aesthetics. The Kindle's innovations in digital ink, book design, and typography are beautiful in their modesty. Bezos was like a digital papermaker, making a product that was at once beautiful and invisible. He strove to create a medium that could enhance the text.

E Ink is an essential component of the Kindle product. Invented by two MIT undergraduates, J. D. Albert and

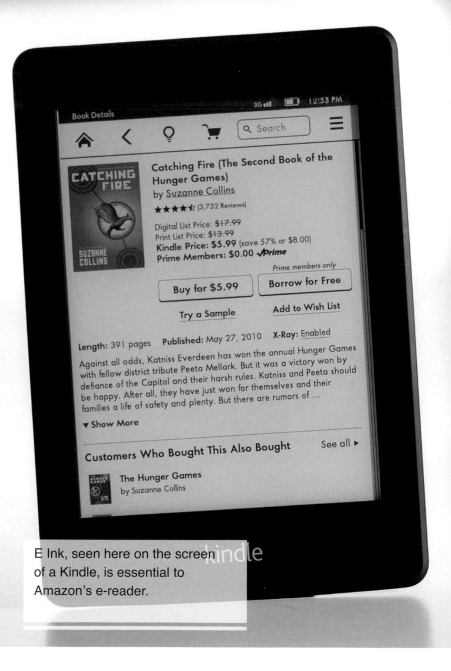

E Ink, seen here on the screen of a Kindle, is essential to Amazon's e-reader.

The LIFE of JEFF BEZOS

Born in Albuquerque to a young mother whose family had settled in Texas and owned a 25,000-acre (10,100-hectare) ranch, Jeff Bezos showed a propensity for engineering and innovation from a young age. He spent summers helping his grandfather on the ranch, repairing fences and fixing windmills. After graduating high school as valedictorian, he attended Princeton University, where he earned two bachelors of science—one in electrical engineering and the other in computer science.

In 1994, as a Wall Street investor tasked with identifying business opportunities in the burgeoning area of e-commerce, Bezos realized that books were the most logical thing to sell over the internet. The two major distributors of books nationwide had already digitized their inventory lists so that bookstores could access them online and order a book for a customer who wanted something they didn't keep in stock. Brad Stone, the author of a profile of Amazon, writes:

> [Books] were pure commodities; a copy of a book in one store was identical to the same book carried in another, so buyers always knew what they were getting … And, most important, there were three million books in print worldwide, far more than a Barnes & Noble or Borders superstore could ever stock. If [Bezos] couldn't build a true everything store right away, he could capture its essence—unlimited selection—in at least one important product category.

Bezos worked on Wall Street using his computer science knowledge, but he soon caught the entrepreneurial bug, and seeing the exponential increases in internet traffic in the early 1990s, he decided that he wanted to be at the crest of that wave. Bezos has worked hard to keep Amazon there ever since.

Jeff Bezos (b. 1964)

Barrett Cominskey, along with their professor Joseph Jacobson, E Ink allows a screen to look like ink on paper, with high brightness and contrast, extremely low power demands, and a wide viewing angle. So unlike your TV, which you can't see well if you're sitting off to the side, E Ink allows the viewer to read the words on the Kindle's screen from virtually any angle, just like a book. E Ink is created by tiny half-white, half-black spheres suspended in a thin layer of oil or **viscous** liquid. When an electrical charge is passed through the spheres, they will turn to either their black or white side. This creates a crisp display that designers of the Kindle use to approximate the look of ink on paper.

According to a study conducted through the *New York Times*, people are more likely to believe a statement if it's written in Baskerville font. Keen to the ways seemingly mundane design choices can alter our perception of truth and reality, Bezos's device used this to his advantage—the Kindle team designs their own fonts. Kindle's font, called Bookerly, was specifically designed to be easy to read, decreasing eyestrain in readers by 2 percent. While that may not seem like a resounding victory, when you think of the goal of Kindle designers—to make their device better than reading a book and never give the reader an excuse to put down the Kindle—2 percent less eyestrain is one of the small advances that the Kindle is staking its future on. If e-reading is to supplant the physical book, it will have to be better, sleeker, faster, and more streamlined than books, which have had centuries on centuries to evolve and improve.

Frontlighting is also an essential part of the Kindle experience. The screen is lit in such a way so that it can be viewed in any light, from harsh sunlight to a dark bedroom. In recent versions, Kindles can auto-adjust for room brightness, so the reader never has to fiddle with the device's settings; the Kindle adjusts itself to its surroundings. The Kindle itself is book and lamp.

RESEARCH BOOKS

Added to give the Kindle a leg up on physical books, X-ray is a program that stores information on characters and locations in a text. When you're reading your Kindle and come across a name you don't recognize, you can simply tap in and a box will pop up telling you who the character is or defining a term. Dave Limp, senior vice president of Amazon Devices, says, "It's a tension between the beautiful but static nature of print, and the dynamism of digital. We're trying to strike a balance between those two things." Amazon is pressing the frontiers of reading forward, so that now the book—if you're reading it on a Kindle— can actually interpret itself, subtly but crucially changing the reading experience. Mysteries in a book—"Where *is* Turkmenistan?"—no longer point the reader outward, into the world outside the book, where the reader must seek the answer from a globe or a friend well versed in geography, but now, through X-ray, these mysteries are solved internally by the book itself.

Amazon studies how people read physical books in an attempt to get to know their competition. They have a plush room filled with comfortable chairs and outfitted with several tiny cameras, where they watch people reading. They've learned that people tend to switch hands about every two minutes, despite the fact that when asked in surveys, they claim to use the same hand. Knowing their customer's hand like, well, the back of their own hand, Amazon added page turning buttons on the right- and left-hand sides of their Kindle Voyager. For a company making an e-reader, Amazon has spent a significant amount of time studying the physical act of reading. But, in the previous chapter, we learned that books have the power to shape consciousness and change minds—it makes sense that the designers of the Kindle would value the physical book.

There are currently six versions of the Kindle. While the technology has advanced, all six versions have a minimalistic design to resemble paper.

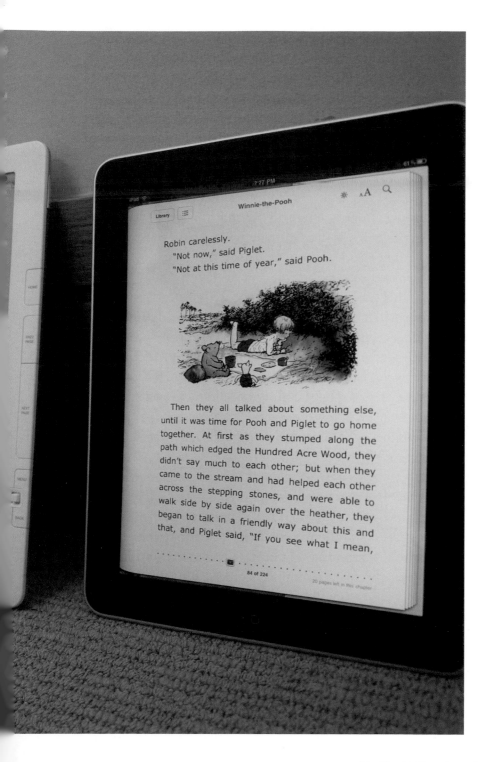

Robin carelessly.

"Not now," said Piglet.

"Not at this time of year," said Pooh.

Then they all talked about something else, until it was time for Pooh and Piglet to go home together. At first as they stumped along the path which edged the Hundred Acre Wood, they didn't say much to each other; but when they came to the stream and had helped each other across the stepping stones, and were able to walk side by side again over the heather, they began to talk in a friendly way about this and that, and Piglet said, "If you see what I mean,

20 pages left in this chapter

For centuries our greatest ideas have been spread through books, and before that, tablets. In order to replace the physical book, it's weight in the hand, the look of paper and ink, the Kindle would need to be very well designed.

The Kindle was made to be a minimal machine, not like an iPhone or other handheld, internet-enabled device. It shouldn't look flashy or draw attention to itself as an object because that would inevitably draw attention away from its purpose—the E Ink word on its paperlike screen. Bezos even mandated that the internet browsing functionality of the newer Kindles be curbed monthly, so while it is very simple to download a book from Amazon's integrated online bookstore, browsing the rest of the internet is difficult. This is because Bezos is not trying to make a do-it-all device like the iPhone, which is a phone, a calendar, a music library, a camera, and a gaming device. The Kindle is singular in its purpose: read and buy books from Amazon. In that, it is perhaps more similar to a print book than it is different. Physical books are generally used for a single function: to read. Bezos's innovation was to see the power and possibility in books and to make a device that tries to match them.

AUTHOR'S PROOF

What do writers think of the Kindle and Amazon's push into the publishing industry? Some think it opens doors for the authors who feel locked out of the exclusive club of the established publishing houses. Meanwhile, others condemn it as the death of literature. Many are deeply ambivalent. George Packer, who regularly contributes to the *New Yorker*, reminds us that:

> In the book business the prospect of a single owner
> of both the means of production and the modes of

distribution is especially worrisome: it would give Amazon more control over the exchange of ideas than any company in U.S. history ... Books remain central to American intellectual life, and perhaps to democracy."

According to Packer, we must grapple with how the wide reach of Amazon gives the company a large amount of control over the publishing and selling of books—of ideas. Amazon is known to wield its power in vaguely Orwellian ways, removing the "Purchase" button from the pages of books published by a house they were in conflict with, for example. With so much power, how can we trust the company to use it fairly?

But for a writer like Amanda Hocking, whose supernatural novels were rejected by publisher after publisher, the self-publishing market was perfect. She has sold over a million copies of her work with Kindle Direct, Kindle's self-publishing imprint. Now she has used her self-publishing as a springboard to negotiate a traditional publishing deal with St. Martin's Press for $2.1 million. And while her personal success is significant, the larger trend is even more so. Books that couldn't get published before—for example, a paranormal young-adult romance like Hocking's—are able to find their audience. The world of literature is becoming more and more diverse, less and less centralized.

NUMBERS and REMAINDERS

Amazon sells 40 percent of all new books in America and two-thirds of all e-books. In a few short years, the company has transformed the bookselling industry, but it also has its sights on changing publishing itself. Self-publishing is a viable industry because of the e-book. It is prohibitively expensive for authors to print, bind, and distribute their own books, because book printing takes expensive machinery and distribution is set up for large publishing houses, not individual writers. But now, because of e-reading technologies, authors can publish their own works online, keeping a much larger proportion of the profits. If an e-book costs $2.99, the author might get $2.00 in royalties, more than half the cost of the book. For a traditional hardcover book, the author may get the same $2.00 in royalties, but the book itself costs $24, with a much larger portion of profits going to the publishing house and bookseller.

The rise in self-publishing has led to a blossoming of genre fiction. Books with a very niche audience— say, a zombie romance or a post-apocalyptic werewolf saga—can be self-published at very little risk to the author, and because they are available to everyone with an internet connection, authors can find their audience instantaneously. Another genre of publishing has exploded thanks to Amazon: audiobooks. In 2008, Amazon bought Audible for $300 million, and the company has recently developed a technology that allows Kindle readers to switch seamlessly between the print and audio versions of a book, so you can read a couple pages on your couch and then resume at the same spot by listening to the audiobook version in your car. This brings up the question: How will we define reading in the digital age? We read so much content every day through the internet and social media, but fewer books than ever. The National Endowment for the Arts found that in 1992, 61 percent of Americans reported they had read at least one book for pleasure that year, while in 2012, only 54 percent responded that they had done so. These are the statistics that the Kindle is hoping to combat; by making the e-reading process as streamlined as possible, they hope to hook readers.

This is not unlike Amazon's broader strategy in e-commerce. Amazon didn't start with bookselling because Bezos considered it a noble profession, but because there are far more books in print than could be housed in a single store, creating a demand for an internet storefront that could send the customer any book. Books are also of uniform size, easy to ship, and difficult to break. Most of all, Bezos saw them as the perfect way to pull in educated customers with disposable incomes, and through their browsing history, collect data on their preferences. This data is very valuable in its own right.

Other companies have tried to compete with Amazon by creating their own e-reading devices, such as Barnes & Noble's Nook. The Nook is the only notable contender, but the device is basically a replica of the Kindle. In order to gain an edge on the Kindle in the e-reader market, the newest device must emulate a book. Amazon succeeded in inventing an e-reader that recreated the reading experience by designing their device to be like paper. However, the Kindle reading experience still leaves a lot of room for improvement: turning the page by touch and scrolling make it difficult for a reader to have a spatial understanding of the text. New e-reader technology should give a physical sense of the book so that the reader feels oriented within the pages and can interact with the text, innovating methods for **e-annotation**, **e-marginalia**, and e-underlining.

The golden proportion, seen in the spiral of this shell, is found throughout nature.

CHAPTER 6
The Power of Invention

Symmetry is a universally recognized standard of beauty. The Korean Hangul script was designed to fit in the outlines of a perfect square, symmetrical in its visual weight. In Japanese culture, white, the color of paper, is also the color symbolizing both life and death. Gutenberg set the dimensions of his book in the golden proportion. In fact, in the narrative of human communication, we see a global symmetry, as many of today's technologies harken back to earlier periods. Writing technologies are an excellent lens through which to view this phenomenon. Writing has become more personal, but also more formulaic. Like in Newton's law, every action has an equal and opposite reaction. As we advance, we also return.

REWRITING WRITER'S BLOCK

In the wake of Kindle's success, a lot of attention was dedicated to the reader's relationship with books. However, digital technology changed the writing process in significant ways, too. Of course, printing on demand and self-publishing changed the landscape for writers, but what about the more intimate place, the place where writing begins? Today, the writing process itself has been altered by word-processing programs. With functions such as cut, copy, paste, and delete, writers can now rearrange and redraft their work without scissors, a jar of paste, and a lot of patience. Because of word processing, generating and editing the content occur simultaneously. While this may seem like a convenience, it's more complicated of an issue than that. Self-consciousness has invaded the early stages of writing; when the "editorial eye" is opened too early, words are erased before they are ever written down.

As cultural critics focused on how the internet age has shortened the attention span of readers, the Kindle proved that readers are out there and hungry for material. The Kindle's technology is intentionally simplified to help distracted readers to focus on a book.

But what about the distracted writer? Is anyone creating devices in the same minimal vein as the Kindle to aid the writer in focused composition? In fact, yes. The Freewrite is a digital typewriter with a screen that allows the writer to view ten lines at a time. The Freewrite does not allow

The Freewrite device's large keys are reminiscent of early desktop computer keyboards.

extensive editing, has no web browsing capability, and syncs documents automatically to the cloud. If we think back to the early scribes and calligraphers, the text had to be perfectly executed on the spot. There was no room for "backspacing" or editing since the materials were costly and not to be wasted. Calligraphers had to get in the proper state of mind for creating text; it was a centered, meditative process. Now, because composing is digital and no paper and ink is wasted if you write seven paragraphs on your computer and then delete them, writing is no longer directly tied to a physical product and process. The writer does not always pay the respect and attention to the process of writing that ancient calligraphers did. We text, we tweet, we delete.

For calligraphers, writing is as much about the process as it is about the product; it was (and remains) a spiritual practice. When you hold a beautiful manuscript, exactingly created by a calligrapher, you are cradling a text where the letters are not simply a transaction of communication, but also a nonverbal expression with a spiritual quality. It is also important because while it is created with precision, the text is also whimsical or ephemeral; the same writer cannot recreate the exact same calligraphy. The physical writing is personal.

Today, handwritten letters are rare, and cursive penmanship is being dropped from school curricula. The physical act of writing is increasingly defined by typing keys. Typed words look no different no matter the writer, unlike handwriting, which is unique to the individual. So while the way we write—physically—is less and less personal, the things we write about, especially when we consider social media, are increasingly personal. Calligraphers would never have used their art to record a "status update" concerning what they had for brunch— calligraphy, because of its complicated and spiritual nature, was reserved for official documents and high art. Today, writing touches every aspect of our lives, from the mundane to the most necessary. We write more than ever before, but the content, because writing is less of a concentrated, artistic effort, has become less essential, even shallow. Now writing is not only valued for its beauty but for its efficiency and ease of use in communicating digitally.

IMMATERIAL READING MATERIAL

Just as the way we write has changed, the way we store and access that writing has also evolved. Increasingly, information is internet based, stored in the digital cloud. But when we say, "Those photos are saved in the cloud," what do we mean? Where *is* the cloud? And how does it function? As in ancient China, where the government was the central holder and distributor of texts and information, today more and more information is being in stored in centralized locations "on the cloud." But despite its misleading moniker, the cloud is not nebulous, free-floating, or in the sky.

Let's take one of the largest providers of cloud computing, Amazon Web Services, as our case study. Following Jeff Bezos's ambition to make Amazon a one-stop shop, they began to build giant data centers, housed in nondescript warehouse-type buildings, filled with football fields of computer servers and elaborate cooling systems to keep everything running. Websites seem like they live "in the internet," but in fact, they must be hosted somewhere, at some physical site—a server where the data resides. The website's data can then be relayed anywhere with an internet connection. Amazon Web Services provides the physical infrastructure for cloud-based companies through their thirty-plus data centers ranged across the globe, so

Information stored in "the cloud" is sent to places like Google Data Center in Hamina, Finland.

these companies don't have to operate their own servers in each location where they provide their service. For example, Netflix is hosted on Amazon Web Services. So whenever you queue up a Netflix movie, your computer is receiving data from an Amazon server location that Netflix has rented.

The list of companies that use Amazon Web Services is extensive, including Coursera, the online open university; Instagram; and PBS. This also means that if an Amazon Web Services data center is experiencing issues, many of the websites we visit daily may have functionality issues or go completely offline, showing how Amazon has centralized the storing of information. The cloud stores art like a museum, collects text like a library, and is also the distributor of those resources. But the physical location— the server farm—is not something you would ever think to visit, and if you did, you would just see stacks of servers with tiny blinking lights, stretching off to the corners of the huge building.

The repository for information has—unlike the library or the museum—become almost imaginary and intangible, and the name "the cloud" obscures the physical site. When you say your photos are in the cloud, that means that instead of being stored on the hard drive of your phone, they are sitting somewhere, perhaps in the middle of Kansas, at a building the size of ten football fields, on a server there, accessible to you through the internet but physically removed. Now, the text and art we create can't be held in our hands, or even contained on our personal devices. It is often stored in "shards," or pieces, diffused across many different server locations, but centralized under one company's—Amazon's—watchful eye, perhaps as divorced as possible from the physical object of the book.

In a perfect twist of fate, a paper mill in Hamina, Finland, has recently been converted by Google to serve as one of their fifteen data centers. This encapsulates part of the evolution of writing. Words, ideas, and art are increasingly stored not on paper in libraries and museums but in digital data centers.

LANGUAGE TAKES a NEW SHAPE

Computer code—a form of writing that is only conceivable in the digital age—is a type of writing even further removed from the human hand. When we discussed paper and movable type, we saw the two as inventions created to serve artists and writers. The invention was a tool that the writer utilized. Now it is almost as if we are circling back to the beginning of written language; when computer code was invented, a new language was formed. But instead of allowing humans to communicate with other humans, as writing did, computer languages allow humans to communicate with machines, using computers or devices as the intermediary between the coder and the human who will use the program created. The printing press is an excellent metaphor for this relationship. We set the press and feed material, blank paper, into it. The machine processes the paper and produces something new: a printed page. In a similar way, the coder writes a program, "setting" the machine, and supplies it with material or data. Then the computer processes it and uses it to create a new product.

The ABC's of 123

Computer code is a major breakthrough in writing. It is the first script that can write independently, without humans. There are many different coding languages, the simplest being the 0s and 1s of binary code. But there are more sophisticated languages that can be layered on top of that, so if you write a program using the coding language C++, for example, the code you write will tell the computer itself how to create more code, down to the basic binary level. Simply put, coding languages can be shorthand for other, more basic scripts, that the computer itself can write.

There are three families of language in computer coding that remind us of the basic forms of communication discussed at the beginning of this book. One is language that serves a utilitarian purpose, like code that instructs the machine to do a very specific task, as in calculating the sum of several numbers. The second type of code is descriptive, like language that is expressive and contained within a community. This coding language describes an object, its patterns of behavior, and its properties. Those are entered, and then the objects interact and are observed. An example of this is computer modeling, like how we use computers to model earthquakes and the damage they might create under specific weather conditions. The last is computer-generated images, or CGI, wherein a computer is used to create and manipulate digital images, often creating works of art. This can be equated to calligraphy, where the writing itself is not simply to communicate but to create images of lasting beauty. Perhaps thousands of years from now, humans will treasure *Toy Story* and its CGI techniques as we do fine examples of Chinese calligraphy.

CREATION and CREATOR

With recent technological advancements, we are closer than ever to an ideal artificial intelligence, as imagined by Alan Turing in 1950. Computer engineers have developed artificial intelligence that can perform a variety human tasks, including making a cocktail, dispensing medication, and harvesting crops. The landscape has also changed for writers: now that new artificial intelligence can write

ALAN TURING: ARE YOU MY MACHINE?

Alan Turing, often cited as the founder of computer engineering, observed that computation was a formulaic and methodical thought process, and he imagined a machine could perform the same function. He developed computer code, a complex text used to make a machine perform a specific function. The software we use for tasks like word processing, reading emails, and buying books online is all possible because of code.

In 1950, Turing published "Computing Machinery and Intelligence," famous for the development of the **Turing Test**, the required standards of a machine in order to be recognized as intelligent as a human. The test is simple. A human sits in a room and is asked to converse with two other subjects in other rooms. One is a human and one is an artificial intelligence program. The original test was performed through typing responses to questions. If the person asking the questions cannot tell which one is the program and which is the other human, the program passes the test and is deemed to have an artificial intelligence equivalent with humans. Computer programmers write the code to create this intelligence, effectively using a language to try to attain "perfection" in passing this test. Like Gutenberg's golden rectangles or Leonardo's study of the proportions of the human form, we are still struggling to define and reproduce perfection, even if the tools we are using are vastly different.

Turing didn't live to see the major developments in artificial intelligence we know today, like Siri or cars that can automatically park, but his ideal machine is still the standard that innovators aspire to.

literary fiction and poetry, writing is no longer a purely human function. That said, the industry needs creative writers more than ever to help develop human-like AI.

Experimental Poetry

it made me want to cry.
no one had seen him since.
it made me feel uneasy.
no one had seen him.
the thought made me smile.
the pain was unbearable.
the crowd was silent.
the man called out.
the old man said.
the man asked.

A common piece of advice that writers pass on to other writers is simple: read. Google, in the beginning of 2016, created a neural network and fed this network three thousand romance novels to improve its conversational skills so it could generate automated email replies for busy people. The program "reads" a text, uses that information to form sentences, and then compares the sentences it wrote to what it read earlier. What came out was not the generally dry, straightforward prose of emails, but something that resembled poetry. In fact, the poem quoted above was written by this program. People began to wonder if artificial intelligence could be used not only to perform functional tasks but to create one of the most human things: art.

In Japan, we see another example of a computer program attempting to create art. Its programmers gave it limitations like specific characters, plot, and vocabulary, then the AI reformulated this input, writing a novella based on what it was fed, titled *The Day a Computer Writes a Novel*. It was entered into Hoshi Shinichi, a literary contest that allowed artificial intelligence as cowriters of entries, alongside many other entries written solely by humans. It made it past the first round of judging, the only one of eleven texts entered coauthored by artificial intelligence to place. The contest was blind, so the judges did not know which works were created using artificial intelligence. Today's technology means that a computer is a voracious reader who writes at a breakneck pace, the author of the future and a programmed poet laureate.

The Novelist's New Narrative

Everyone has that special book. You know, the one that's been read and reread (most likely more than once). The copy is travel-worn and swollen with makeshift bookmarks—scraps of paper, a random bus ticket, perhaps the bookstore receipt from when it was purchased. Sometimes a book is more than just a collection of words. A book can become a dwelling place, a world at once *other* and ours. Sometimes the characters feel so real that, when the book is over, we find ourselves missing them the way we miss a friend who lives in another city. This is the enchantment of reading, when a character becomes part of our life, etched onto the landscape of our mind.

And isn't that the work of a writer: to enchant? Of course, we could say this is true in a metaphorical sense—a reader who cannot put a book down is "under a spell." But now, "bringing characters to life" has a whole new meaning. Tech companies have recently hired contemporary novelists, playwrights, poets, and other writers to create lifelike artificial intelligence characters. Why hire creative writers instead of writers from the tech industry? Because in order to write literature, writers must observe and understand the essence of being a person, the fundamental qualities that make us who we are, in order to portray "realistic" characters (instead of real people). A novelist, for example, does not use conversations from real life for dialogue. Everyday exchanges ("Hi, how are you?"; "I'm fine, how are you?"; "I'm okay, thanks.") are often omitted, even though they are realistic. Dialogue should recreate *how* we talk instead of the things we frequently say.

In order to make these machines seem human, a group of writers and program developers create dialogue, a background story, and personality traits specifically for an AI program. It is because of these writers that most iPhone users know Siri as a personal assistant—one who sends text messages, remembers birthdays, knows where to find the best sandwich in town, has a dry sense of humor, and goes through the occasional mood swing—and not as a Speech Interpretation and Recognition Interface. Perhaps the Tin Man did not need the Wizard of Oz to give him a heart; he just needed a writer to imagine a personality for him.

The FUTURE of OUR PAST

It would be easy to say Cai Lun, Johannes Gutenberg, and Jeff Bezos were inventors—and they were, by vocation. But when we remember that Cai turned raw materials from nature into art when he made paper; that the Forty-Two-Line Bible was Gutenberg's masterpiece; and that by design, the Kindle beautifully recreates a sheet of paper; we cannot dismiss the artistic talent of these inventors. Likewise, writers are not purely artists—to make a painting, the calligrapher must invent his script; to draft a novel, the writer must invent the story. Making art is an act of invention. Perhaps a blurred line separates an artist from an inventor. The two separate entities are linked—makers who seek to remake the world, driven by an impulse to create.

We have seen how writing technologies have circled back around to an approximation of their earliest beginnings. The cloud returns us to a centralized repository of information. Computer programmers write code as scribes invented scripts. The Freewrite device approximates an older form of writing. This return, though, is not a regression but an evolution of the human desire to communicate. As our environment changes and the modes of communication evolve, we find the way we use writing evolving as well. A common thread, though, in this history of writing is the way writing makes ideas physical, turning the intangible into marks on paper. Calligraphy was a way to be a vessel for the intangible, ephemeral meanings the calligrapher sought to capture. Paper was meant to be invisible, not an object of reflection but a way to convey your own reflections. The printing press made literature and the written word personal as people started owning and reading books, writing in them, and becoming attached to the physical book. The Kindle seems like a shift back to the origins of writing, where the physical object is meant to recede—much like paper—and the emphasis is placed on the ideas themselves, e-books stored on a digital cloud, much like the ideas of humanity before writing made those ideas physical. The difference is that today, through internet connectivity, more people are reading than ever before.

But reading and writing are not wholly positive endeavors, according to Plato. If we think back to the quote from Plato in the introduction, he saw writing as possibly deteriorating our collective memories, serving as a crutch. Perhaps we see that today, as people must remember less and less since the information they need is but a few keystrokes away.

Still, there is something necessary about the art of writing.

The Kindle and the Gutenberg Bible were beautifully designed and represent major revolutions in how we read.

GLOSSARY

aesthetic The way something looks; an object's beauty.

calligraphy The art or skill of creating decorative lettering with a pen or brush.

cellulose fiber A long chain of polymers linked by hydrogen bonds, created from materials found in wood or other plant-based materials; cotton, linen, and wool fibers are naturally occurring examples of this, but wood pulp can also be processed to create man-made cellulose.

chih The Chinese word or character meaning "paper."

computer code Numbers that provide information and instructions to computers in order to complete processes.

cuneiform The oldest script in history, which dates back to ancient Mesopotamia. Cuneiform is known for its wedge-shaped characters.

diacritics The symbols for vowels in Kufic script.

e-annotation A note added to an e-book by the author or the reader, including footnotes or links.

e-marginalia A note added to the margins of an e-book by the person reading it.

felted Beaten into a pulp, macerated, and screened, as fibers being made into paper.

golden rectangle A rectangle with sides whose lengths relate according to the golden ratio, approximately 1:1.618, a ratio often occurring in nature and thought to be a divine proportion.

Hangul The alphabet used in Korea since the fifteenth century, where each character represents a syllable.

Hanzi The system of characters used to write Chinese, where each character represents a single word or morpheme.

hieroglyphics A script made from pictographs that was used by ancient Egyptians.

huffaz The term for Muslims who have completely memorized the Quran.

intaglio A description of drawings or characters that are incised and carved into a surface.

kami A colloquial word for paper in Japanese that also refers to divine or spiritual forces.

Kufic An early calligraphic form of the Arabic alphabet, developed in Kufa, Iraq.

language acquisition The human ability to learn and understand language.

logogram A single abstract character meant to represent a word or phrase.

macerate To soften a material by submerging it in water or another liquid.

matrix A mold used to form movable-type letters.

metalloid A metal or mixture of metals.

papyrus Paper made from the reeds of a marsh plant.

phonetic Relating to speech sounds.

pictograph A pictorial symbol representing a word or phrase.

relief Describing drawings or characters that are raised off the surface.

sans serif A font without serifs.

scribe One who copies documents by hand, especially before printing was invented.

serifs Lines that mark the end of a stroke in certain fonts, like the "feet" on an "A" in Times New Roman.

syntax Arrangement of words to form coherent meaning.

Turing Test A test that involves identifying human-generated answers to questions versus the answers generated by a computer.

typography The art and design of type, including font style, size, weight, and layout on the page.

vernacular Languages of particular regions; the term often refers to everyday speech in these languages rather than the formal speech of intellectuals.

viscous A thick consistency between solid and liquid.

washi The Japanese word for handmade paper.

BIBLIOGRAPHY

Basbanes, Nicholas A. *On Paper: The Everything of Its Two-Thousand-Year History*. New York: Vintage Books, 2013.

Battles, Matthew. *Palimpsest: A History of the Written Word*. New York: W. W. Norton & Company, 2015.

Bayers, Chip. "The Inner Bezos." Wired.com, March 1, 1999. http://www.wired.com/1999/03/bezos-3.

Bogost, Ian. "The Future of Writing Looks Like the Past." *Atlantic*, May 9, 2016. http://www.theatlantic.com/technology/archive/2016/05/freewrite/481566.

Brogan, Jacob. "An A.I. Competed for a Literary Prize, but Humans Still Did the Real Work." *Slate*, March 25, 2016. http://www.slate.com/blogs/future_tense/2016/03/25/a_i_written_novel_competes_for_japanese_literary_award_but_humans_are_doing.html.

Brownlee, John. "The Kindle Finally Gets Typography That Doesn't Suck." *Co.Design*, May 27, 2014. http://www.fastcodesign.com/3046678/the-kindle-finally-gets-typography-that-doesnt-suck/5.

Burke, Peter. *A Social History of Knowledge: From Gutenberg to Diderot*. New York: Wiley, 2000.

Burrington, Ingrid. "What People Mean When They Talk about 'the Cloud'" *Atlantic*, November 4, 2015. http://www.theatlantic.com/technology/archive/2015/11/what-people-mean-when-they-talk-about-the-cloud/413758.

Calderhead, Christopher. *The World Encyclopedia of Calligraphy: The Ultimate Compendium on the Art of Fine Writing*. New York: Sterling, 2011.

Cave, Roderick, and Sara Ayad. *The History of the Book in 100 Books: The Complete Story, from Egypt to e-book*. Richmond Hill, Ontario: Firefly Books, 2014.

Drucker, Johanna. *The Alphabetic Labyrinth: The Letters in History and Imagination*. London: Thames and Hudson, 1995.

Gaur, Albertine. *A History of Calligraphy*. New York: Cross River Press, 1994.

———. *A History of Writing*. New York: Scribner, 1985.

Ha, Thu-Huong. "'I Want to Talk to You': See the Creepy, Romantic Poetry That Came out of a Google A.I. System." *Quartz*, May 12, 2016. http://qz.com/682814/i-want-to-talk-to-you-see-the-creepy-romantic-poetry-that-came-out-of-a-google-ai-system.

Hurford, James R. *The Origins of Language: A Slim Guide*. London: Oxford University Press, 2014.

Lienhard, John H. *How Invention Begins: Echoes of Old Voices in the Rise of New Machines*. Oxford, UK: Oxford University Press, 2006.

Man, John. *The Gutenberg Revolution: How Printing Changed the Course of History*. London: Transworld, 2010.

Monro, Alexander. *The Paper Trail: An Unexpected History of a Revolutionary Invention*. New York: Alfred A. Knopf, 2016.

Needham, Joseph, and Ling Wang. *Science and Civilisation in China*. Cambridge, UK: Cambridge University Press, 1954. http://books.google.com/books?id=4z9FAQAAIAAJ.

Newton, Casey. "Inside the Secret Lab Where Amazon Is Designing the Future of Reading." *Verge*, January 17, 2014. http://www.theverge.com/2014/12/17/7396525/amazon-kindle-design-lab-audible-hachette.

Packer, George. "Cheap Words." *New Yorker*, February 17, 2014.

Pilkington, Ed. "Amanda Hocking, the Writer Who Made Millions by Self-publishing Online." *Guardian*, January 12, 2012. http://www.theguardian.com/books/2012/jan/12/amanda-hocking-self-publishing.

Plato. *Phaedrus*. Translated by B. Jowettt. Project Gutenberg. http://www.gutenberg.org/files/1636/1636-h/1636-h.htm.

Robinson, Andrew. *Writing and Script: A Very Short Introduction*. New York: Oxford University Press, 2009.

Senner, Wayne M., ed. *The Origins of Writing*. Lincoln: University of Nebraska Press, 1989.

Stone, Brad. *The Everything Store: Jeff Bezos and the Age of Amazon*. New York: Little, Brown and Company, 2013.

Tsien, Tsuen-hsuin. *Written on Bamboo and Silk: The Beginnings of Chinese Books and Inscriptions*. Chicago: University of Chicago Press, 1962.

FURTHER INFORMATION

Books

Battles, Matthew. *Palimpsest: A History of the Written Word.* New York: W. W. Norton & Company, 2015.

Calderhead, Christopher, and Holly Cohen, eds. *The World Encyclopedia of Calligraphy.* New York: Sterling Publishing, 2011.

Kurlansky, Mark. *Paper: Paging Through History.* New York: W.W. Norton & Company, 2016.

Robinson, Andrew. *Writing and Script: A Very Short Introduction.* New York: Oxford University Press, 2009.

Stevens, Chris. *Written in Stone: A Journey Through the Stone Age and the Origins of Modern Language.* New York: Pegasus, 2015.

Stone, Brad. *The Everything Store: Jeff Bezos and the Age of Amazon.* New York: Back Bay Books, 2013.

Videos

Helvetica
Produced in 2007, this fascinating feature-length documentary explores how typography is created and how graphic design influences and reflects culture.

The Machine That Made Us
This 2008 TV documentary from the BBC explores the life
and times of the mysterious Johannes Gutenberg.

Visions of the Future: The Intelligence Revolution
http://www.youtube.com/watch?v=T9FwxtMgUI8
This first installment of a three-part series produced by the
BBC on artificial intelligence and its current and future
impacts tackles how intelligence and information has
evolved in the digital age.

Websites

The Data Center Mural Project
https://datacentermurals.withgoogle.com/
Google has begun an initiative called the Data Center
Mural Project, which involves pairing with artists to
decorate Google's data centers around the world. This
website includes information about the project, images of
the murals, and a video.

JIKJIworld.net
http://jikjiworld.cheongju.go.kr/app3/jikjiworld/content/
eng_main/index.html
Learn more about the *Jikji* and early Korean printing
methods at the Cheonju Early Printing Museum's website.

The National Art Library Modern Calligraphy Collection
http://www.vam.ac.uk/content/articles/n/nal-modern-
calligraphy
Housed in the Victoria and Albert Museum in London,
this extensive collection of Western calligraphy tells the
story of calligraphy's development in the West.

The People's Cloud
http://www.thepeoplescloud.org
This website contains a series of short documentaries on
cloud computing and images of art installations that use
this new technology as their jumping off point.

INDEX

ABOUT the AUTHOR

Cory MacPherson is a writer and poet currently living in North Carolina. After attending Elon University and University of North Carolina at Wilmington, she received a degree in creative writing. MacPherson continued her study of creative writing, receiving an MFA in poetry writing at the University of North Carolina at Greensboro. A voracious reader, MacPherson's curious spirit fuels her writing.